Cyril Fletcher's Oddities

Foreword by Esther Rantzen

British Broadcasting Corporation

Published by the
British Broadcasting Corporation
35 Marylebone High Street
London W1M 4AA

ISBN 0 563 17940 6

First published 1981

Cartoons by Rod Jordan

Printed and bound in Great Britain
at The Pitman Press, Bath

Introduction by Cyril Fletcher

Every Sunday as I drive from Sussex to London to record *That's Life* I pass a garage with the legend 'Closed 2 stroke toilets'. Do you think they know I pass them every Sunday? Every single post brings photographs and cuttings to my home. *Western Evening Press* – For Sale – 'Pure bred Arab Stallion with good show record and high fertility, present owner unable to do him justice', came this morning. People come up to me as if I were MI5 and whisper out of the corners of their mouths, 'Wot about this then?' and shove a rather bedraggled newspaper cutting into my top pocket and run away. Even quite elderly children of sixty-five do this. Then the next week what do you think happened? I opened a bread roll and there neatly folded as if by a conjurer a headline in *The Sun* – 'Love on a Boat – then P.C. sticks his oar in'. And of course the *That's Life* office receive about seven thousand a week which are opened and sorted by two jolly ladies employed by the BBC. As I undress at night they fall out of my underwear (not the jolly ladies – the cuttings). So really it is in self defence that some of them are reposing quietly, now, here in this book.

But being on the telly brings about the oddest happenings and procedures. If I sit in a low chair to have tea in a certain West End hotel, I am ushered at once into a leather wing chair under a palm in the corner. 'You must have *your* chair,' I am told in thick but friendly Turkish accents by the waiter, who is a *That's Life* fan. I am stopped in the street to be told by quite young mothers, 'My children love *That's Life*, Mr Fletcher, and those oddities you do!!' There is a sort of surprised air to this as if the programme is not intelligent enough for *her* but only her children. 'They should be in bed at that time of night,' I boom, trying to sound like the dear late Gilbert Harding.

Some critics think our choice of cuttings shows an undeveloped schoolboy humour – it's not so much *our* choice but that of the senders-in. On the other hand, this is Sir George Robey's idea of honest vulgarity. It's the kind of humour that used to get a laugh on the Music Halls and a loud guffaw from the supposedly sophisticated audience watching the Savoy Cabaret – I know, I've played both venues many times. It's not a humour of which to be ashamed. Especially if an odd surrealistic angle is added. For instance, from a Cambridgeshire paper came the following offer for sale . . . 'Bed pan £2. Commode chair £2. Crash helmet £7. Wind shield £3.50.' Another jolly little group was found in the *Mersey Mart* . . . 'Three in one, Pram £25, Baby Walker £4, Baby Bouncer £4, Baby £2'. Whereas in the *Manchester Evening News* . . . 'Adults from £45'. Sometimes one hardly believes them like this one from the *Glasgow Evening Times* . . . 'Mr Neilson said today that his department's expenditure has been cut to the bone. He said, "In a situation like that I did not feel I should be circumsized".' But it would be more than our life's worth to fake them or alter them.

But if one is any sort of 'television celebrity' then indeed anything can happen. I opened a Flower Festival at Longleat last summer for the Marquess of Bath. There was a 'ceremony' of a kind at the end of which the Marquess made me a presentation. I have a card by me embossed with a picture of the noble pile and coat of arms.

I quote:

> TO CYRIL FROM HENRY.
>
> ODE DELIVERED BY THE MARQUESS OF BATH – WITH APOLOGIES – TO CYRIL FLETCHER ON THE OCCASION OF THE PRESENTATION OF A LOAD OF RHINO DUNG 25TH SEPTEMBER 1980.

On the back of the card is the ode:

A Rhino isn't like a Rose,
Except, perhaps, its horn
Which grows with pride upon its nose
As a rose will grow a thorn.

So, Mr Fletcher, please accept
A present from a friend
To help to make your roses grow –
Which came from t'other end.

Be careful, for it's very strong,
So each time use a bit;
Please, do accept this Plastic Bag
Of PRIME RHINOCEROS . . .!

In effect, I accepted some rather elegant engraved hock glasses and returned the Rhinoceros manure. But enough of such name droppings!

So let us cut the cackle and cackle at the cuttings.

Foreword by Esther Rantzen

This is an extremely rude book. Cyril has tried, rather half-heartedly, to disguise the rudeness by dotting it lightly through the pages, mixed up with foreign menus and extraordinary signatures. But the fact is that Fletcher's law of misprints says that if it is possible for two letters to be accidentally transposed and turn an innocent phrase into a wicked one, 'cream buns' will become 'cream bums' and an 'audience in raptures' will turn into an 'audience in ruptures'. So if you do explore these pages crammed with the cuttings sent to us on *That's Life*, and you come across some naughty ones, please don't blame us.

Every series, the cuttings we have censored from the programme find their way onto a special noticeboard. That's what makes our office so popular. Senior BBC Executives crowd around it to find the latest misprints, snort with laughter and then remember their august positions and frown disapprovingly. But some of these cuttings conjure up a delightfully fantastic world – robbers who steal chocolate biscuits and macaroni pudding, hooded cows that build nests in high trees. And whenever we take our film cameras out, we discover that the real world is just like that – we find characters like the man who plays *Amazing Grace* on his forklift truck, and a dog who does the washing up.

I am sure you will enjoy Cyril's cuttings and I know we would all like to thank the people who made this book possible – the newspapers who printed the original cuttings, the viewers with such eagle-sharp eyes who spot the smallest misprint in columns of small ads, and the viewers who take a quick photograph of a daft sign and send it in to us. Without them we would never be able to pass these jokes on to you. And if by any chance you find a misprint that makes you blush, please don't blame Cyril or me – blame the viewers who sent us the cuttings we couldn't resist.

Esther Rantzen

What's wrong with food for starters....

CANDIES COOKED BY DIRECT FIRE, THEY DO NOT CONTAIN CONSERVATIVES, ARTIFICIAL COLORING AND FLAVOURS.

DINNER

FRIED SOUP

ESCALOPE VIENESA WITH CAULIFLOWER

PINEAPPLE OR ICECREAM

Σπανάκι βουτύρου
Spinach with butter

Σπανακόρυζον
Spinach with rice

Κουκιά ξερά γιαχνί
Stewed dry horse - been

Φάβα ελαίου
Mashed fava in oil

Μπαρμπουνια — ~~κιλό~~
Mullets — ~~kilo~~

Λιθρίνια — "
Red Mullets — "

Τσιπούρες σχάρας — "
Grilled porgies — "

WELCOMES THE DISCERNING GOURMET

To titillate your palate and satisfy your most demanding tastes, one of Asia's top chefs, Mr. Chow Kum Ming, with more than 30 years experience will prepare for you the finest in traditional Peking, Szechuan & Shanghai cuisine.

Little Juicy Steamed Bums
a favourite of Emperor Chien-Lung's
per tray of 10 Buns: **Only $3.00.**

FOR YOUR FUNCTIONS
* Space for 75 tables for banquets & wedding parties
* VIP Lounge for parties between 10 and 120 persons

Don't be disappointed, make your reservations now
CHINA PALACE RESTAURANT
1st Floor, Wellington Building
Bideford Road (Opposite the Mandarin Hotel)
Tel: 2351365, 2351378

LUNCH

TUNISIAN SALAD WITH TUNNY
or
BRICK WITH EGGS

ooo
COUSCOUS WITH LAMB
or
CHICKEN IN THE SPIT

Potatoes
Vichy Carrots

COLD HORS D'OEUVRE

3,12 Smedovo loukanka-sausage
2,39 Elena pork filet
1,62 Trapesitza rouleau
1,65 Veal soudshouk (sausage)
1,46 Conserved pork filet
1,15 Fumigated sausage
1,15 Choped pork
0,94 Luncheon meat
3,10 Slices of cold meats

C. H. Arrowsmith

Builders, House Decorators & General Repairs

Funeral Director - Cremations Arranged

Also

"DO IT YOURSELF SERVICE"

"CARRS" TAMERTON FOLIOT PLYMOUTH

Your Satisfaction is our Recommendation

6 TON IRON FAIRY CRANE DRIVER

REQUIRED

for Civil Engineers

LADIES, peep in your drawers for any old silver spoons, forks, etc., I will buy any amount, large or small; cash, any condition. Buyer will call

THE MIDDLESEX HOSPITAL
Mortimer Street
London W1

WANTED SPARE RIGHT HAND

MERRY WIDOW REQUIRES MEN. Rehearsals going on now for Easter production, Seaford. Phone Newhaven

THE WIGAN BOROUGH COUNCIL

HIGHWAYS ACT 1959
SECTION 108

STOPPING UP OF LAYLAND STREET AND UN-NAMED BACK PASSAGES, WIGAN

People are still not reading my Adverts properly, when I describe a car as Rust Free I don't mean it hasn't got any rust on it, I mean that any rust that is on it isn't being charged for.

FOR SALE: Gent's upright urinal; also microphone, stand and amplifier. –

And having whetted your appetite, what about a PuPu platter, which as you see will enhance your favourite drink as well

PU PU PLATTER...... Per Person **2.75**

To enhance your favourite drink may we suggest our luscious Pupus (appetizers) featuring the Ding Ho's Titbits of delight (Flaming Hibachi) on a lazy susan surrounded with our assortment of appetizers.

From the *Suffolk Free Press*: 'A "Personal Message" . . . George. I've let the cat out, your tea is in the oven. I've gone to see Charlie, and I will be back in ten years. Amy.' She's Amygrating!

Mrs Thomas from Port Talbot has sent me a notice which her husband, who is a bus driver, received with his wages . . . 'Notice to Staff. I would advise Drivers that there is a toilet facility for Gents only in a narrow lane just opposite the up coach stop in Castle Street, Farnham. This is approximately 80–100 years from the coach stop. Toilet facilities for ladies at this point can be had by using the alleyway by the side of the National Westminster Bank.' There's a terrible overdraft up that alley.

The advertisement of the week appeared in the *Oldham Evening Chronicle*. I quote . . .
'Houses wanted. Oldham, Chadderton, Shaw. Good semi or detached, up to £10,500 required for union official. Must be within striking distance of above areas.'

From *The Times* Births column . . . 'Biss. On Sunday 29th June 1975 to Margaret (née Hunt) and Edgar with thanks to M4 Motorway police – a daughter now at St Teresa's Hospital, Wimbledon.'

And from the *Liverpool Echo*, courtesy of George Sephton . . . 'Taylor, July 1st 1975 to Patricia and George, a lovely son (Robert George). Thanks to wonderful staff at Fazakerley Maternity Hospital and Uncle George from Australia.' Uncle George must be pretty wonderful too!

Report of a speedway meeting as reported in the *Newcastle Evening Chronicle* sent to me by Mrs Jean Kelly . . .
'John Jackson, of Ellesmere Port, the holder of the New National League Silver Helmet, the league's match race title, crashed coming out of the second bend in his first race against the challenger, Newcastle's Tom Owen and was taken to hospital with a damaged leg. The first leg was therefore awarded to Owen on default, and it is hoped that Jackson will be fit enough to contest the second leg at his home track tonight.' . . . and if he loses that one he won't have a leg to stand on.

And finally, a report of a Midland councillor, sadly anonymous, who is reported to have announced to the world . . . 'I find streaking morally wrong. If the good Lord had intended us to run around with no clothes on I'm sure we would all have been born stark naked'.

A soupçon of silly services

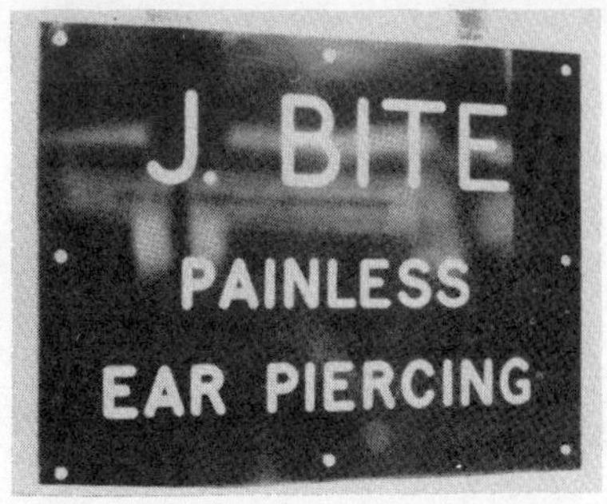

BERTRAM BEES

Because of fat, young Bertram Bees,
Couldn't never not see his knees,
He said, 'Me stomick's spread so fast
They've been hid from view these ten years past.'
Then added, 'It's now my dearest wish,
To shed my excess adipose tish,
I'll no longer be a flabby nit
I'll buy a body building kit.
It seems me diaphragm needs strengthening
Whilst other parts could do with lengthening.'
So off he wrote and bought by post
Exactly what he needed most.
A chest-expander, rowing machine,
And rejuvenating pills for a has-been.
But things went wrong, I'm sad to say,
The box split open on the way.
The postman, after several guesses
Delivered things to wrong addresses.
A fragile spinster called Amanda
Got landed with the chest expander,
And pressing on to her surprise
Got cleavage and two large mince pies.
The rowing machine landed in the hall
Of a man who rowed straight through the wall.
Then battling through the streets with fury
Plunged in the Thames near Mortlake Brewery.
Then flying on with speed and strength
Beat Oxford just by half a length.
A bald-headed neighbour, Colonel Frills
Got the rejuvenating pills,
And feeling cock-a-hoop and frisky
Consumed a month's supply with whisky.
His wife, waking in her bed so snug,
Heard, 'Gooy, gurgle and glug-glug.'

And thinking that she'd really gottem,
Mistook hubby's head for baby's bottom.
He said, 'My dear – please make my happy
And change this goddam awful nappy.'
But poor fat Bert got nothing so,
He wrote to 'That's Life' – now you know.

Northern Western Evening Mail . . . **'Lost in Broughton on New Year's Eve, ladies crocodile, contents of great sentimental value.'**

Havering Recorder, kindly sent to me by Mrs Jill Woods. It's about a dispute concerning the amount of litter in Romford market. A somewhat confused dispute. Romford shopkeepers, it says, have written to the Town Hall. I quote . . . 'We want to find out if the traders aren't the fault of the council workmen who may not litter goes into the council dustcart or if it's Gowland.' How illiterate!

'A group of twelve young American men streaked in St Peter's, Rome, early today. Three were jailed for resisting arrest and committing an obscene cat.' Anonymous viewer from Rome local paper.

Falkirk Herald . . . 'Larbert curling club held their annual dinner dance in the Plough Hotel last Friday. Mr Andrew Robertson was the principal speaker; the reply was by Cyril Prince who had the company in ruptures.'

A bank manager from Leeds sent me an article from the *Farmer's Weekly* . . . 'Learning to Live with the Cow'. And it is not, as you might suppose, about modern marriage, but the Milk Marketing Board's scheme for artificial insemination. I quote . . . 'It is a cheap service. The bull of the day costs only £1.65 and you can't get a man on the farm to do anything at that price.'

Teeside Evening Gazette . . . 'Male members of Cleveland County Council were given a dire warning by Councillor Arthur Seed on Thursday after three councillors were trapped in the gents lavatory. He told the council meeting: "Two members from this side and one from the other were trapped for a quarter of an hour. It was only thanks to the planning department that we got out".'

An advertisement that appeared in the *Wrexham Leader* . . . 'Clever chef meat injector. Stuffs sausages, steak, chops; you need one. Treat the wife. Benefit yourself . . .'

Mr D. M. Wilson of Kingswood, Bristol, drew my attention to the following advertisement . . . 'New Gents Toupees for sale or hire. (CAP) Any area covered.'

Rochdale Observer . . . 'Men wanted for repairing wooden pallets. Also man required for breaking wooden pallets.' I'd like to see the breakdown of the production figures.

Numerous nomenclatures delighted us and the viewers and some were sent by proud possessors of appropriate appellations

'Alf', too, would be welcome and he might even be surprised.

Yours faithfully,
Brigadier P I Attack, MBE
Ministry of Defence
Directorate of Army Management

SURREY EDUCATION COMMITTEE

Report for Term ended Christmas.

Egham St Ann's Heath Council School

E. J. Hale. Form Teacher.
S. E. Clout. Head Teacher.

Affiliated to A.C.U.
Easter Moto Cross
ALSO CORNWALL CENTRE CHAMPIONSHIP EVENT

MOTOR CYCLE SCRAMBLE

AT
POLCREBO, NANCEGOLLAN, NR. HELSTON.

ON MONDAY, APRIL 16th, 1979 at 2 pm

Temporary Track Licence No. 733 Permit No. 0517

OFFICIALS:

Centre A.C.U. Steward E.R.Martyn.
Club Stewards: A. Johns. S. Thomas.
Commentator: B.L.Ellis
Lap Scorers: E. Seymour & Mrs. C.Jenkins.
A.C.U. Examiners: N. Moore & D. Phillips
Gate, Programmes & Car Park Attendants:
Members and Friends of the West Cornwall Motor Club Ltd.
Starter: B. Quick. **Chief Marshalls:** P. Sampson & D. Prowse.
Clerk of the Course: E. Trembath.
Secretary of the Meeting:
B.L. Ellis, Oakland Cottage, Paul, Penzance.

OFFICIAL PROGRAMME (including Admission) **60p**
CHILDREN 10p O.A.P. 30p
The club retain the right to alter or cancel any part of the programme due to circumstances.

Warning ....MOTOR RACING IS DANGEROUS

You are present at this meeting at your own risk and the ticket of admission is issued subject to the condition that all persons having any connection, with the promotion and/or organisation and/or conduct of the mee'ing including the owners of the land and drivers and owners of the vehicles and passengers in the vehicles are absolved from all liability in respect to personal injury (whether fatal or otherwise) to you or damage to your property howsoever caused.

THE CLUB WISHES TO EXTEND ITS THANKS TO THE LANDOWNERS, MESSRS. R. WILLIAMS & F.T. WILLEY.

PART-TIME CLEANERS

required to work mornings, Denbigh area. This work is permanent, not seasonal. The work will be 3 days on and 3 days off which will mean working some weekends.

Apply in writing for interview to:
NORTH WALES CLEANING SERVICES
Mr B. Brushett

6C22D2

F.Perry won nearly everything in the fishing section, and N.Faeber was footballer-of-the-year. Sportsman-of-the-year was A.Goodgame, and Mr Finney presented the prizes.

Freight Transport Association
Hermes House, St John's Road
Tunbridge Wells, Kent TN4 9UZ

To:

B.J.Cork,Esq.,
Bottling Manager
Shepherd Neame Ltd.
17 Court Street
Faversham, Kent

The County Post, *Times-Herald* . . . 'Fire men to show their appliances to passers-by to attract recruits.'

Advertisement from the *Daily Telegraph* . . . 'The Oxford Layhouse Company in *As You Like It*.' Who wouldn't?

'Sid Rawle, 29, part-time gravedigger and editor of an underground newspaper.' He gives the worm's-eye view.

The *Maidstone Gazette* . . . under Lost and Found . . . 'Rochester Cathedral, ninth Sunday after Trinity.' Well, come on. Somebody must have seen it.

Here is the weather forecast as printed in the *Lancashire Evening Post*, Morecambe . . . 'Breezy rather cold but dry and fairly warm.' It's time they started feeling their seaweed.

My thanks to Mrs Choat of West Wickham who has sent me a brochure issued by a local estate agent: I quote . . . 'Do not delay in making an inspection as we are sure you will be very disappointed.' Present owner can't stand the place either.

A correction that appeared in the *Worthing Gazette* . . . 'In our report last week of Davison School PA Fete we referred to Mr Ron Marshall as being the late organiser. This should have read fete organiser. We apologise for the error.' Fete worse than death!

***South Wales Guardian* . . . 'Lliw Valley's development committee have been told that the coming Celtic Sea oil boob is sure to bring benefits to the area.' It's coming ashore in a 34″ cup.**

Some personal advertisements . . . *The Glasgow Evening Times* features the mysterious message . . . 'Mrs Thingy with the maroon Cortina do you still want to sell flowers?' In the *Portsmouth Evening News* there appeared . . . 'Undersealed woman 43 with two children would like to meet gentleman for companionship.' The *Yorkshire Post* carried the following appeal . . . 'Two young ladies after fifteen years working with cows seek change anything considered.' And from the *Birmingham Weekly Advertiser* . . . 'Gentleman 43 interested in gnomes, open cast treacle mining and blotting paper seeks lady with totally dissimilar interests.' He's narrowing the field a bit.

Now we are beginning to find our way about beautifully

CAFE CYRIL
INGLISH SPEA
MENU
R.J.

Which leads us to food again

● FISH FILLETS AND CHIPS

A tasty, quick to prepare combination. Slices of lemon and some parsley make the dish complete.

● PISSOLES AND CHIPS

After you have prepared your chips why not at the same time fry a couple of pissoles while the fat is still hot? Together with some salad, cut-up tomatoes and an egg, you now have a delicious hot lunch.

CAFE BAR ARISTOS

CLASS A' AR. OGIATZIS TEL. 287.467

		WITHOUT PERCENTAGE	WITH PERCENTAGE
Ποικιλία	Various Snacks	[illegible]	[illegible]
Ὀμελέτα τυρί	Omeleta Cheese	10	[illegible]
» πατάτες	» Potatoes	10	[illegible]
Κοκκινιστό	Reddening Meat	[illegible]	[illegible]
Μπριζόλες χοιρινές	Hog Chops	[illegible]	[illegible]
Παϊδάκια ἀμνοῦ	Lamp Shops	[illegible]	[illegible]
Κεφτέδες	Balls of Fortemeat	[illegible]	[illegible]
Ντολμαδάκια	Ball of Rice Wrapped	[illegible]	[illegible]
Μεζεδάκια ἀμνοῦ, συκωτάκι	In vine leaves snacks of livgr		24
Σπλήνα ἀμελέτητα, γλυκ.	Spleen omellet calf pluck		
Κοιλιά τομάτα σπέσιαλ	Bowels tomato special	[illegible]	[illegible]
Γαρδούμια	Gardoumia	[illegible]	[illegible]
Γαρίδες νωπές	Shrimps	—	
Γαρίδες κατεψ.	Shrimps iced		21
Μαρίδες	Small fishes	85	9
Μπαρμπούνια	Red mullers		
Καλαμαράκια	Buttrepishes	[illegible]	[illegible]
Σουπιές	Diferens cuttle fishes	—	—
Ὀκτάπους βραστό	Octapus boiled		
Σαλάτα χωρ. διπλ., φέτα γίγαντες ἐληές	Salad of a village Feta cheese beans olives	[illegible]	[illegible]
Σαλάτα ἀγγούρι, ντομάτα	Salad cucumber tomatoes	[illegible]	[illegible]
Φέτα	Feta cheese	[illegible]	[illegible]
Γραβιέρα	Graviera cheese	[illegible]	[illegible]
Γιαοῦρτι συρωτό	Sour milk (Giaourti)	[illegible]	[illegible]
Σαντζίκι	Satziki	[illegible]	[illegible]
Σαλάτα Ρώσσικη	Russian Salad	[illegible]	[illegible]

Νόμιμοι ἐπιβαρύνσεις Ποσοστόν 15% Δημόσιος Φόρος 5%
Τό κατάστημα ὑπόκειται εἰς ἀγορανομικόν ἔλεγχον.
Legal over charges Percentage 15% Community Tax 5%
This shop is subject to marcet Police control.

WITH HAM-AU JAMBON
MIT SCHINKEN
WITH FUMIGATED SAUSAGE-AU SALA
SEC FUME-MIT SPECKWURST
+LANTSCHEN MIT

EGGS-OEUFS-EIER+OMELETTE:-2 pc
HAM AND EGGS

SCRAMBLED EGGS-OEUFS BROUILLES
RÜHREIER
EGGS WITH HAM-OEUFS AU JAMBON
EIER MIT SCHINKEN
EGGS WITH FUMIGATED SAUSAGE-OE
SALAMI SEC FUME-EIER MIT SPECK
OMELETTE:NATURE

OMELETTE:WITH CHEESE-AU
FROMAGE-MIT KÄSE
OMELETTE:WITH HAM-AU
JAMBON-MIT SCHINKEN
COLD DISHES-KALTE PLATTEN:50g.
CHEESE-FROMAGE-KÄSE

SAUCES:

AS A SPECIAL TREAT TRY ONE OF OUR SAUCES

Chasseur	**25c**	Peppered	**35c**
Monkey Gland	**25c**	Garlic	**25c**
Or a portion of Mushrooms			**50c**

FREDDY FUSS

This is the tale of Freddy Fuss
Who bought a double decker bus
And to his wife, one known as Kate,
Said, 'This will do to live in mate.
No rent to pay — not even fares,
So 'op on quick — get up them stairs.'
They bought wallpaper, paste and paint,
They made it look like what it ain't.
With Tudor beams and plaster pink
All mod cons plus Kitchen Sink.
No 'Mon Repos' upon the gate
They had a destination plate.
And Mrs Fred would lounge in bed
With 'Do not Spit' above her head.
One day when Kate was in her bath,
She thought — 'I'll do it for a larf'
And with abandon — sad to tell
Stretched up her arm and rang the bell.
Her husband in the driving seat
Drove at fifty down the street.
With Katie yelling, 'Stop you beast!'
And soap suds round her Aldgate East.
But on it rushed as buses do
Until a low bridge hove in view.
T'was thus that Kate and Freddy Fuss
Came to own a top-less bus.
In other words at one fell blow
Their bus became a bungalow.
Whilst Katie, nude, without much hope
Tried to camouflage herself with soap.
Yelling to Fred, 'Now you've gone too far
Where d'you suggest I put the loo-far?'
A passing postman, somewhat coarse
Said, 'If she's Godiva — where's 'er 'orse?'

Fred cried, 'Here's *my* boob for all to see
And with yours uncovered that makes three!'
A boy on a push-bike started shrieking,
'Cor! Look at that there lady — streaking.'
The latest news is Freddy Fuss
Now owns a single decker bus,
Whilst Mrs Fuss — his better half
Wears a bikini in her barf.

The *Hendon Times* Group of newspapers published a photograph with this caption . . . 'Mayor carved the ox on Charter Day. In our picture is seen carving the first slice of the late Alderman Bertrand J. Monro.' What a way to go.

Synopsis of evening classes available at the Epsom Ewell and Mole Valley Adult Education Institute. The courses include Spanith, Followed by Speech Therapy.

The Medway Times . . . 'Parkwood Summer Fair. Grand opening by Miss Kent who will (BLANK) in a pony and trap starting at Orchard Street.'

The *Gloucestershire and Avon Life* . . . 'Versatile casual trouser suit by Elida. The jacket has single button cuffs, decorative breast pocket flaps, an optional belt and curved side vents. The trousers are slightly flared and fall straight to the ground.' At the drop of a hat I suppose.

***The Crew Chronicle* . . . 'At the Danebank College of Further Education, Crew, thieves got away with £20 in cash and a chocolate biscuit.'**

I am grateful to Mr Sayer of Chester who has sent me a letter he received from the Royal Albion Hotel in Brighton. I quote . . . 'Dear Sir, We refer to your recent visit to the Royal Albion Hotel and believe that on departure, you may have inadvertently taken away your room. If this should have had happened, perhaps you would kindly return it to us as soon as possible.' Mr Sayer says he's sent their room back but it won't be much good to them, as he's still got the key.

The *Edinburgh Gazette* reads . . . 'Notice is hereby given under the terms of the above regulations that applications have been made to Glasgow District Council Nature of Work Proposed. Removal of Father Will's Organ.'

I've had a letter from a milkman's daughter. She's Miss Valerie Smith of Swinton near Manchester whose Dad, Gordon, had to wrestle with this early one morning . . . 'Gordon. This milk is no use. No. 25 put a note through to say she had got it and you left it Tuesday. I told you to leave it on the 26th which was yesterday and you said did I want it Tuesday and I said leave it Monday so I had to get a bottle. You can leave one sterilised and oblige.'

Some people – Without comment!

BRISTOL'S BIG NIGHT

Valerie Leon, the tv actress who displays, very prominently, as the girl in the Hai Karate tv advert, took time off on Thursday evening to attend the launching of the new BMW Agency at Bristol Street Motors, Southam Road, Banbury.

Valerie is pictured testing the comfort of one of the latest BMW range of cars, with Peter Hill, managing director.

"New puns are welcome," said PC Copp this week.

"I've copped the lot in my time and I've got dark hair so I'm not a fair cop."

What is remarkable is the hole in PC Copp's back garden which, inevitably, he's looking into.

Local historians think it may be an ancient cave but more detective work is required.

MATCH FOR THE LADY CHAMPION

A cross country runner and darts champion were worried recently at Holy Trinity Church, in Roehampton.

The *Burnley Express* . . . 'A Burnley man was remanded in custody for one week by Burnley magistrates charged with having sexual intercourse without consent. He was further charged with causing damage to a table.'

Television review in the *Ipswich Evening Star* . . . 'Most of the sketches were too long and rather lack-lustre. Still, it was harmless family stuff which even the most devout Nun would not object to her daughter seeing.'

From the *Glasgow Herald* came news of Radio Clyde programmes this week . . . 'Seven o'clock, Citizens Advice investigates the problems of sex education. 8 o'clock, stick it in your ear.'

Mrs Thomas in the Rhondda Valley thought this an offer worth passing on to other ladies in South Wales . . . 'Convertible Bed Settee. Also Action Man with accessories.' Handbag and matching shoes of course. Also in Wales Mrs Kelly and Mrs Wollard sent me this reassuring holiday advert . . . 'Pony trecking from the farm on bombproof ponies.' For the sportsman who has everything, Ben Sellens of Highbrook, Sussex, recommends . . . 'Electric Ferret Detector.' From Mr Williams of Wrexham, there's . . . 'Double Bed, low mileage.' From Mrs Gordon of Catford . . . 'Curtains made up a tree.' From Mrs Bladford of Dorset . . . 'Free lay on carpets.' Then for the older man Mrs Fidgen of Worthing offers . . . 'Replacement widows,' or if you prefer it, 'The Merry Window'. Thought you'd see through that one.

Mr and Mrs Webber of Chiswick sent me a report by the Borough Engineer of Hounslow which may be causing some concern to parents in the area . . . 'It was observed that, at this particular crossing, in nearly every case, the time allowed for crossing was adequate but there was great anxiety when the Green Man started flashing.'

From Crediton in Devon, Rosemary Moorhouse sent me this cutting . . . 'Okehampton Spiritual Association – owing to weather conditions and illness the Healing Clinic is closed.' And Keith Edwards of Margate says they have a similar problem in Kent . . . 'Sick Miracle Healer cancels his visit.'

An anonymous viewer in County Down who sent me a report of a council meeting discussing the problems of vandals and conveniences . . . 'The toilet block should remain until we have something more concrete to go on.'

Some places – Without comment!

At a viewer's suggestion I wrote an Odd Ode for the New Year....

As a New Year Resolution, Fred
Said 'I shall stand upon my head,
My friends all think me a clown
But today the world *is* upside down
And p'raps viewed from another angle,
I will understand the tangle,
At least I'll see some funny sights,
Platform shoes and laddered tights,
I'll prove if Scotsmen do wear knicks,
And other undercover tricks.
I'll be upside down and upright too,
Though somewhat bent my worm's-eye view.'

So it was on New Year's Day....
He started the UPSIDE DOWN LIFE WAY.
It was bumpy coming down the stairs,
And awkward sitting up in chairs.
His tea he was inclined to slurp,
He found it inconvenient to burp.
And upside down he found the nation,
Disinclined to conversation,
Although he had a friendly mutter
With a drunken chappy in a gutter.
In the bus queue the stupid feller
Had trouble folding his umbrella,
And a rather common yob
Called him an inverted snob.
He met a friendly doggy
And his bowler hat became quite soggy.

At the office it was not much fun
He was looked down upon by everyone.
He missed his peeps down typists' blouses,
And his secretary was wearing trousis.
Disgruntled he went home again
And his nose holes got filled up with rain.
And with humiliation frowning
Cried 'My New Year's resolution's drowning,
And so shall I if more I sup,
I guess I'll have to turn it up.'
Tritely he said, 'My good idea
Did not prove a panacea,
Whether on your head or heels,
What matters is the way you feels.
Who cares *where* you put your feet or face,
If your heart is in its proper place.'

Department of National Savings Leaflet, Paragraph 11, Revaluation of Contributions . . .
'For the purposes of Revaluing contributions under the terms of paragraphs 7, 8 and 10, each contribution shall be revalued by multiplying its nominal value by the Index figure applicable (as the case may be) to the month in which there falls the fifth or seventh anniversary of the starting date or the date of repayment of a deceased person's contributions (which index figure is in this paragraph called "The repayment index figure") and dividing the product by the Index figure applicable to the month in which the starting date falls. If the Index is revised to a new base it will be necessary, for the purposes of this paragraph, in regard to each contribution made before a revision, to calculate in respect of each of those contributions, and use in substitution for the actual repayment Index figure, a notional repayment Index figure. This notional repayment Index figure shall be calculated by multiplying the actual repayment Index figure by the Index figure applicable to the month in which the revision took place and dividing the product by the new base figure used for that revision for each occasion on which a revision is made between the day following the due date of a contribution, or in the case of a first contribution, between the starting date and (as the case may be) the fifth or seventh anniversary or the date of repayment of a deceased person's contributions.'

In the *Manchester Evening News* an advertisement appeared . . . 'Golden Calf Butcher. Best quality Scotch and English meats free delivery and preparation. Fores of beef, 23p per pound garden gates 18p per pound.'

From the Orkney paper, *The Orcadian* . . . Wedding account, sent by several . . . 'Three of the (bridesmaids) wore plain cream dresses with blue print cotton panels while the small bridesmaid had a plain cream bodice with blue print skirt and frilled hem. They carried bouquets of cream carnations and cornflakes.' The three bridesmaids were called Snap, Crackle and Pop.

Initial Announcements. This announcement appeared in the *Kent and Sussex Courier* . . . 'Greyhound wins darts tournament.' And in an unknown newspaper, an unknown person was advertising as follows . . . 'Wanted – ferret (with or without wooden leg)'. And as if that wasn't enough, the *Carmarthen Journal* featured a Wanted Ad . . . 'Finally Carmarthen pup requires barmaid three or four nights'. Down boy!

STAND CLOSE

NO ENTRY.
FOR BRITISH GAS
VEHICLES
TELEPHONE

LOOSE BOWLS CLUB
FOUNDED 1919
VISITORS WELCOME

FULLY LICENSED
RESTAURANT.
& BAR

VERA SNIGGER

To keep in fashion Vera Snigger
Bought herself a blown-up figure
And thus equipped got much applause
She looked more robust than Diana Dors.
Her husband said, 'Now look 'ere Vera,
Wot is it love – I can't get near yer,
You looks just like a well-fed Venus,
Wot is it that has come between us?'
Young Vera, pleased beyond all bounds,
Increased her pressure fourteen pounds,
And at the garage made folks stare
By calling daily there for air,
At which the attendant, cheeky pup,
Would daily holler – 'Fill yer up?'
Whilst Vera not the least depressed
Entered a Bathing Beauty Contest.
She cried, 'To be the First I must,
I'm going to be the best or bust!'
So getting on a train went she
To the beach of *Much* Dumpling-on-Sea.
Then with ribald cries from bawdy wits
She displayed for all – in starts and fits
Her confidence for all to see,
Her torso with equanimity.
Knowing they would all adore her,
She proudly carried all before her.
The Judge then walked round at leisure,
But had to get a longer measure.
At length he said, 'Well you're the best,
Thirty hips and ninety chest.
No one will beat your shape I guess,
Let me pin this medal on your dress.'
T'was then that things became amiss
For Vera gave a mighty hiss.
The air rushed out as with inner tubes,

And Vera yelled, 'There go me boobs!'
Her husband soothed, 'It's for the best,
Now you have got that off your chest,
Come home with me 'cos now it's plain
You can get in the house again.'
Now as a housewife she knows her station,
Her only dread now is inflation.

Arnold Jones, Shrewsbury, *Shropshire Star* . . .
'The Lord Hill, Shrewsbury. Special Sunday Lunch. Soup of the Day, fruit juice, salad melon, ribs of beef, fresh local roast chicken, stuffed lion.'

***Northern Scot* . . . 'Lost. Strayed from Chapleton, Forres, six BF HOGGS and one BF EWE with twin BF lambs.' Dragging their BF tails behind them.**

Let us now turn our attention to some of the bargains on offer in the small ads columns of our local newspapers . . . Mrs Wooten of Fareham marvelled at this innovation: 'Budgie Cycle, good condition.' Mr Barnes of Brighouse was tickled by the thought of, 'thousands of pool fish for your cricket trousers.' Miss Farrar of Halifax says she is most definitely NOT applying for this job: 'Efficient shorthand typist capable of servicing enthusiastic management team.' My thanks to 12-year-old Natalie Whitehead of Lydney who sent me this ad from the lost and found column: 'Found. Frozen chicken, Worcester Street.' Shouldn't have been out in this weather. And from the pets column my thanks to the hundreds of you who sent me this: 'Large Golden Labrador. Eats anything. Especially fond of Children.' And whilst we're on the subject of children how about this for an offer? 'Super new baby, very good condition £5, Will post.'

Two reports now from local authorities that you might have missed. From near Waddington, Barnsley, details of the South Yorkshire Highways Committee meetings – I quote: 'So the earlier meeting that had earlier been made later was later made earlier because of lateness.' Thought you'd like to know that. And Peter Adam of Westward Ho sent me this good news from the Wessex Water Authority . . . 'Bath, known the world over for its Spa waters now claims to have a better class of sewage.'

My bargain of the week came to me from the Students of Swansea Art College . . . 'Six million dollar man £4.50.'

My thanks to Mrs June Wise for sending me this warning for children in the Bristol area – keep away from The Molehouse at Clevedon where they serve 'Superb traditional Sunday lunch with a choice of roast beef, lamb, pork, chicken, with reductions for children because they cook quicker.' Cot Age Pie? Get it? Cot . . . age . . . Oh why do I bother?

If you are unemployed some of these jobs may still be vacant

BRA STAFF

Part-time and evenings, excellent remuneration for affable experienced persons.

Please apply to:
Mr G. Spencer,
Fox & Hounds,
Enfield Green,

EXCITING OPPORTUNITIES FOR SALES STAFF WITH KNOBS AND KNOCKERS

The specialists in door furniture and fittings, opening shortly in Debenhams of Harrow.

Excellent career prospects for an experienced manager, and full time and part time sales persons. We offer rewarding salaries, commission scheme and staff discounts.

Tel. the Personnel Department

No doubt you'll need a holiday by now

SELSEY £12,000 Offers. Horrendous holiday home of slum-standard construction and offered in appalling condition.
Make early appointment to view before the whole property collapses.

FAMILY HOLIDAYS, with personal service catered for in June, early July and August, only 10 years from beach,

HOME FROM CANADA

After three interesting and enjoyable wees in Canada. Mr. and Mrs. Vivian Rees. Brynamman-road, Lower Brynamman have arrived home.

Wisbech Advertiser . . . 'The bride was attended by Mr McPhee who wore a brown two piece suit with pink head piece.' Probably caught the bouquet as well.

The *Bexhill-on-Sea Observer* . . . 'Normans Bay level crossing will be closed to traffic for the next three weekends while railway engines repair the road.' What clever little puff-puffs.

The *Wolverhampton Express and Star*. I quote . . . 'Walk out dustmen go back . . . Dustman Wally Evans was suspended after a row with a councillor's daughter. She claimed he had been abusive to her. But he said that was rubbish.' Well, it probably was.

What has been happening in the world of showbusiness? Mark Northall who is 14 and comes from the West Midlands recommends his local cinema which is showing: 'Kink Kong'. Nick Stock of High Wycombe says he thoroughly enjoyed this week's edition of 'Crassroads'. Keith Randall of Romford was glad to see they are brightening up Sportsdesk *on Radio 2 with songs from Roy Castle, the Nolan Sisters and Barry Mason. And Mrs Lena Matherall of Wantage, Oxfordshire, thought Lulu was a bit mean with her fans when she gave them each a SINGED photograph of herself.*

Northamptonshire Chronicle and Echo. I quote . . . 'He decided to go fishing on the day of the incident – August 24 last year and caught a bus.' Fares please, mind the jaws.

The goings-on in the Council Chambers around the land. For instance, E. H. Humphrey of Newton Abbott, South Devon, sent me the following cutting from his local paper . . . 'Both Councillors advocated that action was needed to control dogs and clean up the streets. To brush it under the carpet as we have done for the past 30 years would be wrong, said Councillor Mrs Rooke.' And at a meeting of the Newport Town Council, Shropshire, I quote . . . 'Town Clerk, Mr Doug Keddir, said anyone wanting a mug should get in touch with him.' And in the valleys of Wales they have a couple of real spoilsport councillors called Ray Davies and Colin Hobbs who have written to transport manager Mr Des O'Sullivan condemning the decision to take all BUSTS out of operation at lunchtime. Rotters.

News from the Press Association . . . 'Some bread delivery men have begun boycotting shops and supermarkets selling LARGE LOVES for less than 19p.'

Or some more permanent accommodation

STEYNING. A well-maintained Semi-detached Edwardian House near Steyning High Street. Elevated position and bay windows give magnificent views of the single gentleman tenant in the ground floor apartment, the remaining two floors consist of kitchen, bathroom, separate w.c. and 4 spacious bedroom / reception rooms. There is a long, attractive garden, car standing and car port could be constructed at the side of the property. Redecoration and a little attention to the condition of the interior is required; the exterior has recently been refurbished. **£15,000** Freehold.

157, CARTMELL ROAD,
WOODSEATS,
SHEFFIELD, 8

THIS IS A WELL MODERNISED MID-TERRACE PROPERTY WHICH HAS HAD CONSIDERABLE WORK DONE ON IT IN RECENT YEARS, INCLUDING FITTING OF A BATHROOM AND RE-WIRING APPROXIMATELY EIGHT YEARS AGO. THE PROPERTY STANDS IN A CONVENIENT POSITION, BEING CLOSE TO LOCAL SHOPS, SCHOOLS AND BUS SERVICES AND WITHIN EASY REACH OF SHEFFIELD CITY CENTRE.

Viewing: The property may be viewed strictly by telephone Telephone Chesterfield 810243.

HENRY SPENCER & SONS

ABERAERON

Very pleasantly and conveniently situated in this popular seaside and harbour town within easy reach of all shops, schools, etc. The —

Freehold spacious, Double Fronted Georgian Stone and Slated 5 Bedroom, Fully Centrally Heated Residence with Walled Garden and Rear Access off Service Lane.

1 BELLE VIEW TERRACE,
Aberaeron, Dyfed

Is offered For Sale by Private Treaty (or Public Auction at a later date) with Vacant Possession on completion by arrangement or instruction of Mr. and Mrs. L. B. Jenkins.

Apply:
EVANS BROS.,
Auctioneers and Estate Agents,
1 Market Street, Aberaeron (Tel. 570462)

Viewing: By arrangement via the gents only.

Solicitors: Messrs. J. Gwynne-Hughes & Son, 26 Alban Square, Aberaeron.

HASTINGS outskirts. — Choice of two first-floor flats in mansion-type conversion with panoramic views; large lounge, bedroom, bathroom and kitchen; common use of large delightful gardener - maintained grounds; £8,000 each. — [illegible] &

For the convenience of Prospective Purchasers wishing to view by lorry alternative arrangements can be made with the Office Bike.

KIDDERMINSTER. [illegible]
A printing error last week caused confusion, the price for this martly podernised semi-detached horse in an excellent situation is £9,750. Most convenient living accommodation with recently installed bathroom and wc, three bedrooms above. Long garden with open rear outlooks. Freehold. To view please contact this office.

Reports of activities on the wedding front. Mrs Garner of Bourne End sent me a cutting which described the bride's attire as follows . . . 'She were a long plain white vile polyester dress.' Otherwise she were lovely. Then there was Mr Marmanfarmai who wore 'a brown chiffon velvet gown.' I'm sure he looked lovely too. And for the bride-to-be, R. G. Claxton of Kings Lynn in Norfolk, has sent me the following bargain: I quote . . . 'Beige maternity dress, size 16, worn once for wedding.' The shotgun's extra.

Television page of the *Derby Evening Telegraph* . . . 'BBC-2 8 o'clock, Menuhin: A celebration of his 60th birthday opening with a performance of Mozart's Violin Concerto. 9.30 The Man Alive Report on the Fiddle.'

Birmingham Post . . . 'Eric Skeels, Stoke's 36 year old defender has been given a free transfer. He played only four first team games this season after struggling for long spells with knee and thing injuries.'

Stains Informer . . . 'Room Decor. Venetian and vertical blonds supplied and fitted.' A sort of blind date?

Benn Sewell of Greenford sent me a copy of the Safety and Welfare report issued by his firm. I refer to an accident that occurred on the seventh of April . . . CAUSE 'Slipped on wet floor, knee struck ground. Action Taken – Floor checked to see if damaged. Operator told to be more careful.' Stupid boy.

A piece of advice now for the gardeners amongst you. Mr Ives of Enfield sent me instructions he received on how to look after trees. I quote . . . 'As these are trees they are hardy to look after outdoors. If kept *indoors*, ensure that your tree is not exposed to heavy rain.'

Golf International . . . 'Shameful Saunas. In view of the recent adverse publicity in connection with saunas and massage parlours. We at Eurogolf would like to make it quite clear that in none of the saunas in establishments featured by us will there be any such nonsense or messing about, and for this we would like to apologise.'

Various members of the congregation of St John, the Baptist Church, Bere Regis in Dorset wrote to tell me of their concern about their vicar, the Rev Paul Tranter, who in a letter beginning, 'My Dear People . . .' signs himself, 'Your sincere fiend and vicar.'

More cannibalism

NEW GROUP product manager at KP Foods is John Koster, previously with Kentucky Fried Children. Mr Koster joins the KP Nuts team and his responsibilities will include KP Disco's.

Chicken Fricassee & Chasseure
Grilled Gammon Ham
Grilled Lamb Chop
Grilled Pork Chop
Grilled Sausage (2) and Bacon ASC
Sausage Lyonnaise ASC
Grilled Lover and Bacon
Kidneys (Saute) ASC
Grilled Tomato (1) (Fresh)
Fried Onions
Corned Beef Fritters
Pies - Beef and Potatoe ASC
Beef and Kidney ASC
Beef and Vegetable

Brush chicken joints with a little melted butter and grill slowly uhtil golden brown and tender. Drain pineapple rings, pouring the juice into a small pan. Add orcestershire sauce, pinch dry mustard, salt, Cayenne pepper, and bring juice slowly to the boil. Blend cornflour to a paste with a little cold water and add the juice, stirring. Return to the pan, bring back to the boil and allow to simmer.
Brush pineapple rings with butter, grill and place on a warm serving dish with the chicken. Cook the peas and arrange on serving dish. Coat the children with sauce and serve.

----------oOo----------

LARDED AND STEWED POPE'S EYE
WITH MUSH ROOMS
Maitre de Hotel Potatoes
PIG'S TROTTERS TROPICAL STYLE
COLD BUFFET

Vegetables and Vegetarian Specialities 81

Mashed Potatoes **6 minutes**

toes of any size, milk, butter, salt, pepper.

Cut potatoes roughly into 2·5 *cm* (1 *in*) chunks and pressure steam in separators for 5 to 6 minutes. The smaller the potato pieces, the more rapidly they will cook. There is no need to season at this stage. Place cooked potatoes in mixing bowl and mash by hand, using the remaining steaming fluid and/or milk to moisten the mix, if required

***Western Mail* . . . 'Sports Blackout. France's state-owned television network yesterday cancelled live transmission of two major sporting events, the Spanish Grand Priz and the Rome International Horejumping.'**

Capt. S. Pangalos of Ealing, London W.5, sent me his parish magazine, *The Ascension Herald*. Under the heading Young Wives Group I quote . . . 'May we remind you again of the first coffee meeting of the summer session which is at Angela Barnett's on Tuesday, May 4th. Other husbands are invited to an exciting wife and coffee tasting evening.' Grounds for divorce?

Mr Gaunt was a milkman in Staleybridge, where the Fivepenny Piece come from, and the notes he got left in the morning explain a lot. All completely genuine. This one, from a lady: 'Please don't leave any today as I have two in front.' Congratulations Madam. And congratulations also to the customer who left this note . . . 'Please leave five bottles of milk. We're at it again. Thank you.' You're welcome. And finally: 'Will you please bring a small carton cream on Wednesday and leave it halfway up my passage.'

***Kentish Times* . . . 'Sausage selling vicar's wife wanted for a similar promotion in Sidcup.' The dog-collared them.**

Mrs F. Mottram of Pudsey sent an extract from a set of instructions she acquired in Greece for dancing the Syrtaki . . . 'The dancers, one near the other, take each other from the shoulders. The left foot goes dragging forward and the right foot follows – also dragging. Then the right foot goes dragging forward and the left follows also dragging. All this with the dancers body forward. Then the left foot goes one step left and the right follows at the height of the left foot's fingers. The left foot goes one step ahead, and then the right behind the left one, crosswise. The left foot one step left and then the right one in front of the left crosswise. The right foot right one side step and then the left in front of the right crosswise. The right foot towards the right and the left in front of the right crosswise, then the right one step right sidewise and the left joins. Then . . . two local jumps, and then one jumped step towards left (the left foot backwards and the right forward) and one towards the right (the right foot backwards and the left forward). The music becomes quicker. The right foot makes a shocking step ahead and the left follows in a shocking manner, then the left smoothly backwards and the right follows towards the right, and then the left comes in joining and so on.'

There's no business like show business as portrayed here

CHESHAM LIGHT OPERA COMPANY

PIDDLER ON THE ROOF

Elgiva Hall, Chesham 18-23 April

Tickets from Elgiva Hall Box Office Tel. Chesham 74759

Geisha Night Club

At the 12th floor overlooking a Magnificent, Scintillating view of Cairo by Night is the "GEISHA" A Dance Band and an Oriental Dancer creating an Atmosphere of "A Thousand and one Nights" dont miss it . . .

Take the Elevator and Press the 12th Bottom

NOW !

For your Diner we sugest . . .

"l'Entrecote GEISHA"

MANCHESTER ROAD COMMUNITY CENTRE

AFTERNOON TEA DANCES

COMMENCE TUESDAY, OCTOBER 4th, 1977

2 pm

Admission 20p

(including flea and biscuits)

D-I-S-N-E-Y W-E-E-K

Monday, Tuesday, 27th and 28th

Walt Disney presents

ONE HUNDRED AND ONE DAMNATIONS 8.55.

WEDNESDAY NEXT, April 18, at 2.30 & 7.30

THE BOURNEMOUTH OPERATIC SOCIETY in

I ıtr-duced by GORDON HONEYCOMBE

Proqramme includes excerpts from "My Fair Lady." "Merry Widow," "Showboat," "Pink Champagne," Song of Norway"

BOO NOW ALL SEATS £1.00 (mat only OAPs 60p)

BERTHA BOOT

This is the tale of Bertha Boot
Who bought an opaque bathing suit
That means when wearing it in water
You don't see things you didn't oughta.
The girl who sold it her said, 'Madam
If Eve had worn this suit for Adam
He'd not have seen her tit for tat
Or apple dumplings come to that!'
Now this pleased Bertha on the whole
Because she was a modest soul,
Who felt she should pull down the blind
Before she even changed her mind.
Whilst birds and bees meant in her view
Some honey and an egg or two.
She said, 'I'll give old Fred a laugh
And wear my opaque in the bath!'
Their courting had been almost cold
Their engagement had been six years old,
Till one night in a forest glade
She let him see her shoulder blade.
Now Freddie was her happy spouse –
Don't switch off Mrs Whitehouse!

Then in her bath to make Fred giggle
She gave her extremities a wiggle,
And looking up saw goggle-eyed
A window cleaner perched outside
Who, at the window made a lunge
And rubbed his cloth and squeezed his sponge.
For through the wet suit for all to see
Came Bertha's shining modesty.
Thinking her costume was opaque
She gave a sexy shimmy shake
And leaping with a merry stride
She flung the bathroom window wide.
The window cleaner with glazed eyes
Said to her in some surprise,
'Cor lumme, ain't you never saw
A window cleaner bloke before!'
Her husband Fred came in that minute
It's funny how fate times things init?
Seeing her husband she cried, 'Old Fruit,
Do you like me opaque bathing suit?'
Fred thinking her in the altogether
Started humming 'Stormy weather'
'That's not opaque,' he said all gruff,
'You're standing brazen in your buff!'
So Bertha still for all to see
Rushed from the room all H & C.

From the *Bolton Evening News* . . . 'Young man, 26, wishes to meet young lady, aged 26/30. View to friendship and outings. Well reared Kennel Club Registered.'
Got a wet nose as well?

The *Newcastle Champion* . . . 'Working class man in thirties would like to meet a woman with fat legs for friendship and marriage.'

Belfast 'News Letter' . . . 'In recent years two new species have penetrated the boundaries of the city. The collared dove which first appeared in Belfast in 1964 and the hooded cow which not only breeds in our parks but is building nests in high trees.'

***Carmarthen Journal* . . . 'Diane Dunbar School of Building and Plastering – Ballet Classes.'**

Births Column of the *Bournemouth Evening Echo* . . . 'Martin. The Warren, 14 Mitchell Road, Canford Heath. To Bunny and Doey, the arrival of fourth bunny, Baby Buck (Stuart). Ferret wanted.'

The *Yorkshire Evening Post* . . . 'Will the gentleman who borrowed a donkey from Scarborough Sands please return it as the season has started.'

Chester Chronicle . . . 'Thieves broke into a house in Northop recently and stole items worth more than £260 including a television set, sheepskin rug and a tin of macaroni pudding.'

The *Bristol Evening Post* . . . 'The day after a butcher joined the staff in the Tesco Supermarket in East Street, Bedminster, a series of thefts started. They were from the pockets of employees hanging in the staff rest room.'

Cheltenham Echo . . . 'Situations Vacant . . . Special Women and Girls required. We have full time and part time vacancies – Crumpet Department.' I prefer fluffy pastry.

A caption in the Ministry of Agriculture's Journal *The Bulletin* . . . 'Professor Heslop-Harrison receiving the plague from Baroness Birk.'

The liquids have become oddities here, to say nothing of the entry requirement, and then with 'Kettle or Fish', 'Mussells at the vapour', 'Pyjama', 'Laytart at the Wishky', 'Lambs Chop at the burning wood', and finish with 'Whore Rib Beeb' — how shocking. One wonders does Aunty know?

opening hours
8.30am - 9pm mon - fri
9am - 5pm sun
9am - 9pm tue

customers must show their ass
before being served in this restaurant

SOUP
KETTLE OR FISH
ONION SOUP
LEMON SOUP
ANDALUSION COLD SOUP
MEAT'S CONSOME WITH YOLK OF AN EGG

SALAD AND HORS D'OEUVRESS
MIXED SALAD
VARIED HORS D'OEURESS
COKTEL OF GAMBAS
ASPARAGUS WITH MAHONESA
AUCLADO PEAZS WITH GAMBAS OR VINEGAR
MUSSELS AT THE VAPOUR
CATALONIAN SPINACHS

MEAT
ENTRECOT, Speciality of house
STEAK AT THE BEPPER
WHORE RIB BEEB
ESCALOPE OF PORK
ESCALOPE CORDON BLEU
LAMB'S CHOP AT THE BURNING WOOD
LOIN OF PORK WITT PORK
FILLET OF VEAL GRILLE
TORNEDEO ROSSINI
DUCK TO THE ORANGE
CHICKEN BREAST SAUCE ES[illegible]
CHICKEN AT THE RED WINE

DESSERT
FRUIT AT THE TIME
ORANGE'S ICE CREAM
LIMONADE'S ICE CREAM
PYJAMA
CROCANTI
EGG'S CUSTARD
ICY TART AT THE HISHKY
MELON WITH ICE CREAM
FRESH WATER MELON (at the [illegible]
CHEESE OR MAHON
ICE CREAM
CAKE, Speciality of house

FLUMMERY

Ingredients:
½ pint fine oatmeal — Soaked overnight
2 pints water — Soaked overnight
2 blades mace
½ nutmeg, grated
½ pint white wine
2 teaspoons orange flower water
Method:
1. Soak the oatmeal in water overnight.
2. Strain and add two blades of mace anc
3. Boil for 15 minutes.

Frugal Irish stew

Metric	*Imperial*
Large breast of lamb, on the bone	*Large breast of lamb, on the bone*
450 g onions, peeled and sliced	*1 lb onions, peeled and sliced*
1 kg potatoes, peeled and sliced	*2 lb potatoes, peeled and sliced*
Salt and freshly ground black pepper	*Salt and freshly ground black pepper*
225 g carrots, peeled and sliced	*8 oz carrots, peeled and sliced*
1 × 5 ml spoon chopped fresh thyme or ¼ teaspoon dried	*1 teaspoon chopped fresh thyme or ¼ teaspoon dried*
Water	*Water*

Sign here....look whose signature is at the bottom of the page

2... that all current planning Permission granted under the 1963 Act continues in force for five years from said 1st November 1976 so that in this case Outline Planning Permission granted on the 1st April, 1974 now remains in force until 1st November 1981.

Trusting I have made the position clear.

Yours faithfully,

ensure that all cheques are duly cleared before being forwarded rselves.

Yours faithfully,

P.G Bogle.
Group Financial Director.

I remain,

With kind regards,

Ruud Kok
exportmanager.

ration in this matter will be appiecated.

Yours faithfully,

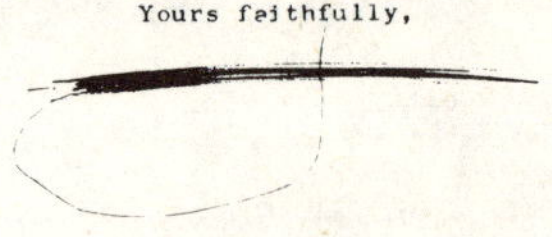

S.R.G. NKAPHAZO NGIBO

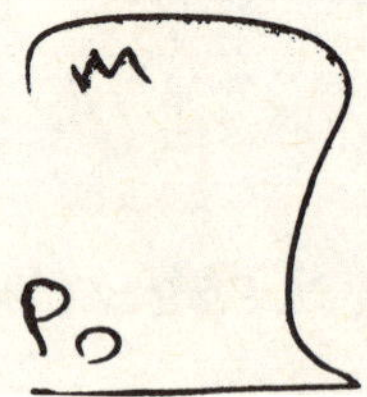

Copies have also been sent to G.K.N. BIRWELCO

Yours faithfully,
Bureau Technique Jean DENIS s.a.
L'Administrateur - Délégué

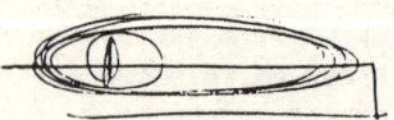

Mohamm ad-Pournazari

Yours sincerely,

ALAN ELDERFIELD
Publisher.

thanking you for your enquiry, we assure you of our tention at all times.

Yours faithfully,

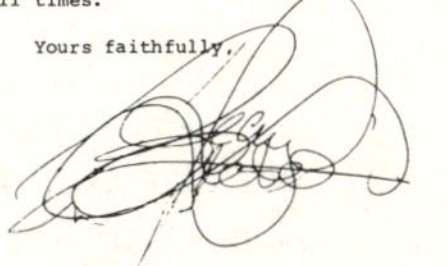

B. Meeres
for(District Manager

ss, sign and return to us as soon as possible.

Assuring you of our best attention at all times.

Yours faithfully,

Michael C. Edwards.

Yours faithfully,

R.L. Grabham
Branch Manager

Yours faithfully,
P.H. Haydock & Co. Ltd.

C. Moon
Sales Office Manager.

h considering local conditions, the self-drive car should be

well in our Incentive Scheme. I trust that more of you will
nmission. Have a good season !

Hugo Amaya-Torres (*Managing Director*)

it but perhaps later.

earing in my One Man Show at the Key Theatre,
n August 13th if you'd like to come.

Yours sincerely,

Cyril Fletcher

Weekend Magazine – a column called Pets Clinic. I quote . . . 'I am breeding rabbits and would like to show them but have no experience. How do you advise going about it?'

The Cardigan and Teivyside Advertiser . . . 'The secret of a beautiful carpet lies in the fitting. Make sure you get your next carpet fitted correctly by entrusting the job to a qualified carpet fitter – to a man who can supply the highest references. Get it fitted by Frank Evans, Pantolwen Vach, Gorrig Road, Llandsill. Fitting service for stairs, room, halls, landings, cowsheds.' And make sure the cows don't drop ash on it.

***Farming Life* . . . 'The Black Abbey Herd has to offer at Balmoral 1 bull and 1 heifer. The heifer is from a 2,000 gallon cow and the bull is the daughter of an R.M.X.'**

Helen Sangster sent a copy of the typed prospectus for Hounslow School . . . 'Boys in transition are not allowed to wear trousers without permission of the Headmaster.'

Mr H. G. Foulger sent a series of advertisements that appeared in the same issue of the *Eastern Daily Press* . . . 'Blackcurrant pickers wanted at Hemblington . . . Christopher Wace, Gables Farm, Come to Hemblington . . . Strawberry picking . . . Christopher Wace, Gables Farm; Owing to a very heavy crop of strawberries we need still more pickers at Hemblington . . . Christopher Wace; Pick your own strawberries and gooseberries at Hemblington . . . Christopher Wace . . . Fruit picking is finished at Hemblington for the season. Christopher Wace thanks everyone who has helped.'

***Leicester Mercury*, concerning the retirement of a local schoolmistress, Mrs Jans. I quote . . . 'At a presentation held in the village church Mrs Jans was given a tea-set and a travelling rub by the vicar.'**

The Law Society's Gazette . . . 'A. I. Brodkin practising as Adrian and Company is pleased to announce that as from 1st of May 1975 he has taken into partnership his wife Diane B. Brodkin with whom he has been associating for some time.'

13-year-old Keith Harris sent me the following advert from Gillingham . . . 'Skilled body repairer required to operate busy-body shop.'

Here are an odd collection of activities and entertainments

AN ILL-WIND

AS A MAN walked out of the Cantilever Garden Centre, Latchford, his jacket was blown open by the wind and revealed a floral arrangement valued at £19.25p, Stockton Heath magistrates were told on Tuesday.

THURROCK CONSERVATIVE ASSC

RECEIPTS AND PAYMENTS ACCOUNT FOR THE

Cash in hand and at Bank 1st January 78

Subscriptions

Profits on wine evening, cheese and wife party

Profit on barbeque

Profit on May morning

Eastern Evening News, Friday, March 12, 1976 11

Empty your cesspit over the phone.

DRAINAGE DEMONSTRATION

CANCELLED

Unfortunately the drainage demonstration which was to be held at Woodton on May 19th has had to be cancelled due to wet site conditions.

A History Making Event is taking place in your Town

B. H. T. Doulatram & Co.

THE MOST DISTINGUISHED DEPT. STORE

proudly Announces

Christmas SALE

No body have dared to slash prices in

THE BARBARIC WAY

COME • BE CONCEIVED

B. H. T. DOULATRAM & CO.

48/50, High Street, 2 Floors. Tel: 37846

We start with a reception at the Guinness Depot in Apollo Road, off Boucher Road, of Stockman's Lane, near the MI in Belfast. "Elevenses" will be supplied from about 9.45 and also a glass of sherry or beer. Toilet facilities will be available and loudspeakers will keep us all informed as to what is going on. Southern entrants will leave from Kevin Sherry's garage in Monaghan as usual.

'Womancraft' article about bee-keeping and the health of bees . . . 'To keep a check on the health of your bees you can take advantage of a free health service. The secretary of your local bee keepers association will give you the address of the centre nearest to you. Send a matchbox full of dead bees and you will receive a detailed report of the state of their health.'

First Aid advice – Bolton Handbook, was sent to me by Mr Tait . . . 'Check 1: Is the casualty conscious? Talk to him, if he replies he is conscious. If no reply he is unconscious.'

Let us see now what has been on offer in the small ads column of our weekly newspapers and magazines. From Mrs P. Stacey of Watford . . . 'Lost. One man's black handbag in Watford High Street.' Tony Croft of Falmouth offers the perfect retreat for Mrs Thatcher . . . 'Hall, Lounge, Dining Room, Two conservatives.' From Andrew O'Brien of Ilford . . . 'Wicklow, Britas Bay, mobile hole to let, sleep 8.' From Mrs K. Marshall of Liverpool . . . 'Home for horse with shorthand typing.' From Eileen Mason of Littlehampton . . . 'Gardener to work part time in dental practice.' From Jimmy Murdock of Glasgow . . . 'Environmental Protection Services, professional control of rats, mice, insects and priests.' From Eric Gom of Hern, Kent . . . 'Lot 94, 2 upholstered armchairs in tweed and a loose lover.' From Tom MacDowell of Bristol . . . 'An American Company needs a secretary with *farst* accurate shorthand' – and the ability to spell is essential. And from Margaret Butler of Oxford . . . 'Manure, well rotted, bags supplied, do it yourself, cheap.'

Warrington local paper . . . 'Irish Terrier Bitch 6 months old, kennel club registered, £20 to good home only. BLEEDER emigrating.'

Mrs N. Hague of Northallerton who sent me this excerpt from a holiday brochure she has been reading. It extols the virtues of the volcanic Greek Island of Ios . . . 'Even the windmill in the village which looks like it stepped straight out of a "Come to Greece" guide book is for real, grinding corn for a living and not just reserved as a tourist attraction. The wizened old miller will gladly show you the interior, single ladies negotiating the rickety stairs getting a friendly grope to speed them on their way.'

And where better for entertainment than TV — some programme notes!

7.30 — **Feature Film:** The Robe: starring Richard Burton, Jean Simmons, Victor Manure, Michael Rennie.

7.55—The Master Game.

8.25—In Search of Offa.

9.00—Call my Clugg. (New series).

9.30—Cricket: Third Test.

5.15 **NETWORK**: From BBC Northern Ireland: A chance to live — why so many babies in Northern Ireland die or are handicapped.

5.45 **HORIZON**: Where Nothing Happens Twice. Repeat.

6.35 **INDOORS OUTDOORS**: Expert cooking, gardening, do-it-yourself

8.45 News. weather.
8.55 The Lively FArts: Dave Brubeck at Symphony Hall.
9.40 Murder Most English. A Flaxborough Chronicle, starring Anton Rodgers, part 6: Coffin. Scarcely Used.
10.30 Screen 2: A Day in the Death

9.0 A Party Political Broadcast

9.10 Call My Bluff

11.00—What's It All About?

11.30—Executive Suite. The Rules of Seduction, followed by Bedtime and Closedown.

4.45 **EASTER MATINEE.** "Cry the Beloved Country" (1952), starring Canada Lee, Charles Carson and Sidney Poitier. Screen version of Alan Paton's famous plea for racial harmony in South Africa. A white and a black man have one thing in common—they each have a son (not in colour).

★

6.15 **IN DEEPEST BRITAIN.** "Orkney."

FREDDY FORRY

This is the tale of Freddy Forry
Who was in need of a new lorry
On which to load his cod and skate
And drive them back from Billingsgate.
His wife said, 'Fred, why don't you try
A little bit of D.I.Y.?'
'Do it yourself,' said Fred, 'That's me,'
And wrote off to the factory.
He decided as he'd got no shed room
To assemble the lorry in the bedroom.
So planks and screws and wheels galore
Were then delivered to his door.
And staggering up the stairs he'd say,
'Come on Amelia – out the way.
Don't want to catch you unawares
Me big end's coming up the stairs!'
'If that's your big end,' said his wife,
'I'm learning things too late in life.'
One night in bed she threw a fit,
She'd sat upon his brace and bit.
And said to Fred, 'Now Freddy what'le
I find next, your blooming throttle!'
And fumbling underneath the sheet
Found his sparking plug complete,
She said, 'You are a funny bloke
I much preferred the old two stroke.'
Until through April's hazy gloom
A lorry stood inside his room.
His wife woke up and vaguely said,
'Coo lumme, what you done there Fred?'
'Stand by,' said Fred 'and Tally-ho!
Eyes down, stand clear and 'ere we go!'
And leaping in the driver's seat
He pressed the pedals with his feet.

At which the lorry gave a jerk
Charged madly on and went berserk.
Crashed through the wall and down the stairs,
And caught the postman unawares.
Who, as he fumbled with a letter,
Got two bricks up his carburettor,
The house, not equal to the strain
Will never be the same again.
But Fred's wife said, 'Well, have a try –
We'll build a new house, D.I.Y.'
Later, Fred, a clumsy fixer
Fell into the concrete mixer.

I have two interesting jobs to offer now. From Robert Dundas of Caithness . . . 'WANTED Company Director making small profit seeks rich widow as sleeping partner.' I expect he runs a bed and breakfast establishment. And from E. J. Glendenning of Falkirk . . . 'Miners Drawers required, apply to Mr. Smellie.'

Some reports from this week's sporting press. From Mr K. Hewis of Bournemouth . . . 'Chris Old the England fast bowler may miss Yorkshire's match against Northants at Middlesborough. He infured *his* at Arundel.' Poor chap. And on the rugby field, Paul Carpenter of Croydon sent this report . . . 'John Lloyd caught a university forward on the wrong side of a loose moll.' And C. Hewitt of Worthing sent this soccer report . . . 'Kidd was sent off in City's 4–0 defeat at Derby following a souflee with Steve Powell.'

For all those people born under the sign Aquarius . . . 'As the day works through, your finances are going to look a little healthier and by evening you may be ready for a bit.'

Selection of small ads from local papers and magazines. From D. Bunce of Hampton Wick . . . 'Horse manure by the sock.' Sock it to me baby. From Richard Blaydon of Bristol . . . 'Sincere lay seeks residential post.' From 12-year-old Glenda Thompson of Runcorn . . . 'Members of Hillside W.I. organised a mumble sale.' From Marie Wormold of Leeds . . . 'Part time physiotherapist. Hours by arrangement but some on call CUTIES will be necessary.' From Mrs Drury of Cromer . . . 'Teacher needs shooting, can you help.' From Miss Mills of Exeter . . . 'Hedge Trimmer, Black and Decker £5 used one season. No hedge now.' From Judi Pickering of Wellingborough . . . 'Cot Italian style, large baby to *ding*.' From Ron Harding from Trowbridge . . . 'Doors, staircases, *widows* etc. *made* to order.' From Mrs O'Hagan in Windsor . . . 'Weeding Dress Size 12.' And from B. A. Calderwood of Stamford . . . 'Square toilet tent for sale. Trumpet in case.' In case the door won't shut, presumably.

My award for the best headline to come my way goes to Mrs Anne Wijec of Arbroath, Scotland. It reads . . . 'Man Found Dead in Cemetery.'

An advertisement that appeared in the medical magazine, *Pulse* . . . 'Doctor's wife makes ideal birthday gifts, woollen womble type figure, three feet high.' Never mind, dear, personality counts as well.

Who, I wonder, is likely to answer these advertisements

CAN YOU PEDAL A TANDEM BIKE
thru Westwood dressed as an
A V O C A D O
Part-time promotion work
AM & PM $3.00 per hr.
479-8197

3005 EAST FRANK PHILLIPS

FROZEN FOOD DEPT.
OLE SOUTH
FROZEN
COBBLERS
Big 2-lb. Each 97¢
BIRD'S EYE

SPANISH SATSUMAS
CLASS I
8 FRUIT
PACKED BY SUPERIOR
BISHOPS GR 94

PRELIMINARY
FOR SALE BY PUBLIC AUCTION
(No offers prior to Auction)
WEST CRAIG
ST JUDES

ON THURSDAY, JUNE 14, 1979
at 11.00 am on the premises.

Smallholding with attractive Residence in elevated position enjoying panoramic Southerly views together with approx. 26 acres land, out-buildings and large pong.
Advocates: Messrs Dickinson, Cruickshank & Co, Water Street, Ramsey.

ONE SIZE
100% ACRYLIC
MACHINE WASHABLE
WARM FUMBLE DRY

BIRP
FOR RELIEF OF
FROTHY BLOAT
400ml.

3ft. Wide **COMBINATIONS** Sliding Door for Easy Access . . . . FROM **£45.95**

Selection from the small ads columns of the weekly newspapers.

Bargain of the week came from Mr Heslop of Skipton . . . 'Three foot children's beds from £2695, cots at £3700, four foot six divan sets from £5350.' And then they have the cheek to say Beat Inflation, Shop with Us.

Then from Mrs McNeel of Doncaster . . . 'Two ladies blouses, bust 38″, one blue, one pink.' One hot, one cold.

From D. Cliff of Sale . . . 'Camp bed and lightweight sleeping bog.'

From Christine Lloyd of Bromsgrove . . . 'Electric Foster Mother, thermostatically controlled.' Hot stuff that.

From Graham Perry of Harpenden . . . 'Cortina MK II 1967 reconditioned engine new front legs.'

From Mr Nunn of Wokingham . . . 'Men's digitals, £5.50.'

Clare Dunston of Chichester . . . 'Ear Piercing while you wait.'

For the cockneys amongst you Karen Gibbs offers . . . 'Rice horse trailer.'

Here's a posh one from Alexandra Grant of Putney, Richmond Hill . . . 'Elegant spacious self-contained flat on 3 floors, gas central heating – hitting room.'

And Mike Hutton of Market Harborough sent this warning to Farmers. I quote . . . 'Farmers, book now for shearing, fott trimming, castrating and de-horning.'

My award for the Best Service of the week goes to Smith and Grieves, Builders and Decorators of Upper Norwood. I quote from their invoice sent to a customer . . . 'Raised ladder to rear main roof, so as to clear blocked hopper, removed small section of zinc to enable us to get access into hopper. Found that the blockage was caused by a very dead sparrow, named Bruce, removed same, gave kiss of like but to no avail, replaced zinc and left hopper and down pipe clear and free running. No charge.'

And here's an offer many of you may find yourselves unable to refuse. It comes from M. J. Holland of Leicestershire . . . 'Owing to the sale by the present owners of Sezicote Stud, the entire staff will be available to take up new positions at the end of the present stud season.'

We've left these hors d'oeuvres for a final course!

7 UP Ox sport Cola ... 21 ~~25~~
Orange juice ... 25 ~~30~~
Mango ... 25 ~~30~~
Gripe fruit juice ... 25 ~~30~~
Tomato juice ... 25 ~~20~~
Mineral Watear : Evian & Vittle ... 75
Turkish Coffee ... 22 ~~18~~
Tea ... 26 ~~15~~

MEAT DISCHES : Cordoun blow - 225

Fillet Paprika ... 200
« « with Mushroom ... 225
« « Grilled ... 178 ~~155~~
Homburger with eggs ... 95
Eescalope pannee ... 145
« Paprika with Mushroom ... 198 ~~180~~
« natural ... 145
« milanaise ... 180
Lamp shops ... 150

CHICKEN & PIGEON

Roated chicked or Pannee (Half) ... 171,5 ~~150~~
Paprika « « ... 171,5 ~~150~~
Roasted Pigeon ... 90
Grilled « ... 90

DESSERT :
Rice Pudding (oven) ... 25 ~~20~~

Lunch & Dinner Obligatory
SERVICE 10%

Rice

Macaroni

Onions

Mad balls and sau.

Mousaka

Ribs 10.00
Eggs of Adult Ox — in Extent 10.00
Sheep in Oven 400
Lung in Sauce 400
Beef in Sauce
Foot in Sauce
Beef Soup
Bean Soup 25.00

Great Beginnings

Prawn Cocktail ... 85
Egg Mayonnaise ... 62
Smoked Mackerel ... 55
Grilled Fruit Juice ... 25

PORRIDGES:

Of vermicelli. ... 12
Fishing porridge ... 19
Hen's porridge ... 12
Porridge with egg's yolk ... 16
~~Spanish rice~~ ...
Green beans with potatoes ... 24

FISHING

Sea's spider to the furnace ... 44
Mayonaise lobster ... 95
Large sea craw-fishes ... 60
Repleted calamaries ... 44
~~Russian sauce~~ Lobster a la americana - 110
Boiled merluce with mayonaise ... 55
Merluce with asparagus sauce ... 59
Fried merluce with lemon ... 54 ~~48~~
Merluce chins in green sauce ...
Cod "a la vizcaina" ... 46
Tunny with tomato ... 45
Fried red mullets ... 45
Sardines ... 30
Pollock to the furnace ... 65
Sole ... 65

PROCESS WORKER

We require a person in our Wokingham factory to be trained to take over the processing of the famous Ex'Lax Chocolate Laxative, preferably experienced in the food or pharmaceutical industries.

We offer a good salary to the suitable applicant plus a friendly working environment in a small subsidiary of the Culbro Corporation of the USA.

Please apply to Mr Pile

EX'LAX LIMITED
Fishponds Road, Wokingham
Telephone Wokingham [illegible]

GYMNASTICS WOMEN SUB. 2

BUL	035	RAHNEVA, ANTOINETA
BUL	037	VARBANOVA, KRASSIMIRA
BUL	036	TONEVA, KRASSIMIRA
BUL	034	GEORKEVA, IRENA
BUL	032	TOPALOVA, SYLVIA
BUL	033	GLOUHTCHEVA, DILIANA

P.G.A. Member

Golf Foundation Registered Coach

Professional

Falkirk Tryst Golf Club

DONALD SLICER
86 BURNHEAD ROAD
LARBERT

Telephone Larbert 2091

RELIEF MILKER

ON REGULAR PART-TIME BASIS TO MILK TWO HERDS OF 60 AND 100 COWS AT BUCKLAWREN FARM, ST. MARTIN-BY-LOOE TWO OR THREE DAYS PER WEEK.

Telephone:

D. J. BUCKETT

Mr. D.M. Snapper,

B.D.S.LOND.,L.D.S.,R.C.S.ENG.

DENTAL SURGEON.

MR. B FLAT
BAND INSTR. REPAIR

disposed of in a proper manner."

Mr P. Nutt, who runs a vet's practice in Ramsbottom and Bury with his wife, Hazel, said: "I must admit that I have not studied Mr Holt's letter, but from what I can see,

MR. N. E. MEANEY.

WAGES INSPECTOR.

Name of the game

Councillor Alf Sparkes has stood down as Wyre Forest Council's representative on the Midlands Electricity Consultative Council.

But Councillor Bill Fish will remain on the Wyre Forest Youth Angling Association.

ARGUE & PHIBBS,
SOLICITORS

I am writing in the hope that you may f
local News Programme. I hope that the
needs.

Yours faithfully,

Mr. H. K. Grubb
Catering Manager Sub Group

CRASH
SCHOOL OF MOTORING
D.o.E. Regd Instructors
Dual controls
BRAINTREE 25371

MINISTRY OF DEFENCE
(PROCUREMENT EXECUTIVE)
ROYAL SIGNALS AND RADAR ESTABLISHMENT

CANTEEN ASSISTANT

A vacancy has arisen for a part-time Canteen Assistant at the Royal Signals and Radar Establishment, Baldock.

The successful applicant will be required to work approximately 20 hours a week.

Please apply to:—
Mr R. D. Kilham,
MINISTRY OF DEFENCE (PE)
RSRE BALDOCK
HERTFORDSHIRE SG7 6NG
(Telephone Baldock 893355)

Parachute Regiment, Bruneval Barracks, Aldershot, were remanded on bail at Aldershot on Wednesday.
They are: Michael Dropinski (19), David Wilson (30).

G. F. B. PULLAR B.D.S. (Glas)
Dental Surgeon

ART PRINTERS and
STATIONERS

TELEPHONE BELFAST 25524
Reid & Wright
SHAFTESBURY HOUSE . 62 CLIFTON STREET . BELFAST BT13 1AB

Sillitoe C, 6 Alton Rd.......... .... W
Sillitoe C.T,State Regd Chrpdst,
155 Burnage La 19..
Sillitoe D.W, 158 Warwick Rd,Weston.........Macc

THE OBSERVER'S BOOK OF

MUSIC

By
FREDA DINN
G.R.C.M., A.R.C.M., A.T.C.L.

Illustrated by
PAUL SHARP
A.R.C.A., A.T.D.

DACAP Expansion Continues!

FIELD SERVICE ENGINEER
(Male/Female)

required for electronic cash registers and P.O.S. systems. Should ideally be living in Dundee, to repair and maintain installations in East Scotland.

Previous experience with T.T.L. and C.M.O.S. microprocessor technology is necessary.

Estate car provided together with usual progressive company benefits.

Write or telephone with brief details for application form to

BUNNY LABBETT, Field Service Manager,
TRANSACTION DATA SYSTEMS, LTD.,
Dawlish ..., Devon DX7 0NH.

Birmingham Post . . . 'Mr Karnane, a factory worker, who was one of the elected delegates said that the people elected were not Left Winkers.' I'm glad I got that right, you should have heard it at rehearsal.

Report in the *Telegraph* about MP's and dental workers telling the Royal Commission on the Health Service that many unnecessary fillings were given and that teets were being damaged by dentists. They knew their drill!

Try the Hilltop Motor Hotel, Carlisle and let me know if they live up to their promise, I quote . . . from their brochure . . . 'When we say welcome, we mean it and we bend over backwards to make you feel it.'

Time now for my selection of small ads from your local papers and magazines. From Mrs Hazlett of County Antrim . . . 'Trousers, latest style with flared TURNIPS.' Or if you prefer it . . . 'Tomato PANTS 13p each.'
And to move your produce around the garden Brian Turner of Reading suggests . . . 'Really immaculate very fast wheelbarrow many extras £380.'
Doreen Bennet of Havant likes . . . 'Chamber pot with large cacti.' G. Jones of St Annes on Sea recommends . . . 'The bottomless dancer and supporting shorts.' Mr Male of Bolton liked . . . '5 lbs of MICE £2.'
The sparks must have been flying in Chingford this week . . . 'WANTED IN CHINGFORD LIVE ELECTRICIAN.' And I can't imagine what's going on in Berkshire where Dennis Hall has drawn my attention to the Marlow Bottom Plumbing Service.
But my award for the vision of the week goes to Barry Hewitt of St Albans who spotted this outstanding offer . . . 'Girls brushed nylon pyjamas. Bust 432 inches.'

My saddest cutting came from Mr D. G. Baker of Birchington, Kent, and concerns the Great Debate on Education. I quote . . . 'And Kenneth Turner, a spokesman for a parents group revealed : apathy among parents is a problem. We organised a discussion on apathy but nobody turned up.'

WE DON'T have all that many compliments but today a casual customer brought back a cream bum commenting that it tasted bad. It was one of the buns that Mick our local baker, brings every day and for which we have a good sale.

"What's the matter with it?" I asked.

"It tastes funny," said the customer.

very little. And this brings me to the final stage and the most unhappy one of the dilemma in which we find ourselves in connection with Professor Constable." He produced a number of typewritten sheets which he opened and began to thumb through, peeeing at them once over the tops of his glasses.

There was now a rustle and a quickening of interest on the part of those gathered there and Hero inferred that all that had been said and taken place before had not touched any of them deeply, but that which

"I find streaking morally wrong. If the good Lord had intended us to run around with no clothes on I'm sure we would all have been born stark naked."

Delays on the line

NO TRAINS will run between Redhill and Tonbridge this Sunday and delays of up to 30 minutes can be expected.

A £12,000 blaze which destroyed a wooden store at the South Hants Sun Club nudist camp at Boarhunt has left the owner with no private possessions.

There a welcoming party, including manager Mr Rodney Widdowson, and Grill Room manager Mr Carlo Ambrosini, popped the first cork to toast the vintage.

The wine was escorted from Dover by Mr Peter Chaning-Cotter, Cafe Royal deputy manager, and Mr Martin Mislin, of the International Food and Wind Society.

"Anyone who knows these pubs knows there is no vestige of truth in the suggestion that they cater for homosexuals. Their biggest customers are probably sailors."

WILLIAM WOSSAGE

This is the tale of William Wossage
Whose Basset Hound was known as 'Sausage'
Because as William quaintly said,
'This flipping dog of mine's half-bread.'
But Sausage, needing much correction,
Was *not* a model of perfection.
As a football fan he caused dismay
'Cos he did his summer pools each day
And worse than that, the silly hound
Chewed everything that could be found,
Odd letters lying on the mat,
Galoshes and a bowler hat,
A rolled umbrella of the vicar's,
Elastic from the barmaid's knickers.
Nothing was safe from this mad pup
He just sat down and tore 'em up.
At last poor William blew his top
He said, 'This lark has got to stop.
The barmaid says I'm a disgrace
And waves her bloomers in my face.
I've had to beg the next door's pardon.
He's been careering round their garden.
I reckon this will mean a fine
He's come back with the washing line.
3 vests, 4 pants wrapped round his shoulder,
2 roll-ons and a dumpling holder.'
His wife said, 'Now I think that's rude,
And I do not like your attitude!'
'It's not my 'at 'e chewed,' said Bill,
'It's your 'at off the window sill.'
One week-end at a Labour Rally
Held by the Party at Ally Pally,
He caused a yell from Barbara Castle,
He sank his fangs in her metatarsal!
One afternoon – now do not mock

He swallowed the cuckoo from the clock
And all day long he'd perch himself
And cuckoo from the mantel shelf.
They got the vet to come next day
The reason was, I'm sad to say,
They thought they'd all go crackers 'cos
The cuckoo kept asking what time it was.
Then, looking grave, the kindly vet
Said, 'I'll operate, with much regret.
And lest he swallows aught else rummy
Put a zip fastener in his tummy.'
The strangest of tales then the telly told,
They wonder what will his belly hold?
They open the zip, whilst he wags his tail,
And they send what they find to a jumble sale.

David Barrow of Halifax sent me this information about an injury in his local football team. I quote . . . 'Terry Gennoe broke his nose while trying out his fractured little finger.'
Pick of the week, no doubt.

Miss Vanessa Kiddle of Stevenage who gave me some advice on what to take rock climbing . . . 'A Williams site harness, helmet, 13 chocs, seven slings, pitons, 22 krabs, one pair of goolies size 45.'

A selection of ads from local papers: Mrs Doreen Mowbray of Cheltenham sent this one . . . 'Siamese kitchens for sale.' Slant eye level grill of course.
Mrs Shepherd of Swindon sent me . . . 'Pair Red Rumps £14.'
Mrs Bradford of Cobham offers . . . 'Raymond 21 inches, not working, some parts missing, £5 or nearest offer.'
Donald Mackay of Glasgow likes the sound of . . . 'Modern mistress with high pressure boilers.'
But if you're looking for something a bit stricter, Margaret Jones of Sutton Coldfield suggests . . . 'Governess for sale. Chassis OK, body needs some attention.'
Mr Clarke of Grimsby sends . . . 'Small lock up shop (ex cobblers) on corner of Willingham Street (facing Mecca).'
From the Anniversary columns Diane Lloyd of Grantham liked the silver wedding greetings to Nana and Grandbag.

Turning our attention to the countryside, my thanks to Mr A. J. Morton of Scotland for drawing my attention to the following advertisement . . . 'Shepherd/Stockman required for Laghead Gatehouse who or when available. Blackface sheep and suckler cows occupy farm house.'

Mr Petch from Aldershot liked the sound of Mrs Marjorie Cawthorne, who according to the local paper 'is the warden of theeheeheeheeheeheeheeheeheeheeheeheeheehee homes.' And another merry story from the same paper involved a charity walk . . . 'There will be no stopping at pubs along the way for this group of regular drinkers from the Prince of Wales in Ash Road, Aldershot. "We'll get a lot further if we don't stop at pubbebbesebsshshshsh".' Cheers!

WANTED EXPERIENCED BELLIE KNOCKER, good pay.

A BABY SITTER AVAILABLE,
Babies must be dropped & picked up by parents. Reasonable monthly charges. For further details Please Ring

WANTED: Messenger. Must supply own bike and own messages.—Phone Shaemus at home KP8/5

MARRIED LADY dental surgeon, age 42, very little experience, would like 4 or 5 sessions a week.

TIRED BUSINESSMAN
requires
SLEEPING PARTNER
TO INVEST SOME CAPITAL AND HELP WITH BOOKWORK
Genuine
Accounts available
Pleasant office
Write J 45, JEP

FLAT CIRCULAR MECHANIC WANTED

An experienced knitting Technician/Mechanic with good all round knowledge of yarns and machinery for development and production on Flatbed and Circular machines. This is an interesting and responsible position with attractive salary.

Write or phone for appointment Managing Director
JERSEY LOMAX LTD.
MORRIS ROAD, LEICESTER — TEL. 705058

OFFICE PERSON

with good telephone manner and ability to work on own initiative required to work in site office in Avonmouth.

Own transport desirable, salary negotiable, successful applicant will be required to share gent's toilet. For interview:

OLD LADIES WANTED

with

Twisted Legs, Brass Dials, and wooden trunks

Sporting fans, I'm sure, will be interested in this report of a rugby match sent to me by Mr Carson of West Lothian. I quote . . . 'The game got off to a quiet TART.'

British Airways have been having a spot of bother.
Mrs Sheila Gorman of Dundee sent me details. I quote . . . 'British Airways shop stewards met today in a bid to resolve a dispute which has strangled thousands of passengers at Heathrow.'

Yorkshire Evening Post . . . 'A young lady wishes to meet wealthy gent in poor health, view to long lasting friendship.' And in Plymouth Mrs Baker is not going to apply for the job she saw in her local paper – under domestic it said 'Cleaners required for male areas.'

Sunday Telegraph . . . 'Bristol's first League win of the season was a triumph for teenager Kevin Mabbutt who skilfully scored one *gal* and initiated two more.'
He obviously knows how to make a pass or two.

Margot Brampied sent me the programme for an agricultural show in Guernsey in which the last award was . . . 'The Mardon Trophy Cup, presented by Mr Dennis Norris for the cow with the best udder in memory of Mrs Frances Pittard Norris.'

***Jersey Evening Post* . . . 'World's most exclusive car for sale – it has carried only royalty and celebrities' dung.'**
Phew!

Farmers Weekly . . . 'For sale. The Devonian Ewe Truss used by satisfied shepherds for 50 years.'
Now we know what ramshackle means.

I expect many of you will have heard about Mrs Mary Whitehouse's new book in which she poses the question 'Whatever Happened to Sex?' Well, I think Mrs Celia Bowditch of South East London might have found the answer at the Peckham Film Theatre . . . 'Super Saturday Show for boys and girls, 9.30 a.m. DIARY OF A SPACE VIRGIN, FORMERLY THE SEXPLORER.' And I used to waste my time watching Roy Rogers and Trigger.